JOURNEY
under the
Sea

Linda Pitkin

OXFORD

For Brian

OXFORD
UNIVERSITY PRESS

Oxford New York

Auckland Bangkok Buenos Aires Cape Town Chennai
Dar es Salaam Delhi Hong Kong Istanbul Karachi Kolkata
Kuala Lumpur Madrid Melbourne Mexico City Mumbai Nairobi
São Paulo Shanghai Singapore Taipei Tokyo Toronto

Published by Oxford University Press, Inc.
198 Madison Avenue, New York, NY 10016

www.oup.com

Library ISBN 0-19-521971-6

Trade ISBN 0-19-521972-4

1 3 5 7 9 10 8 6 4 2

Printed in Hong Kong

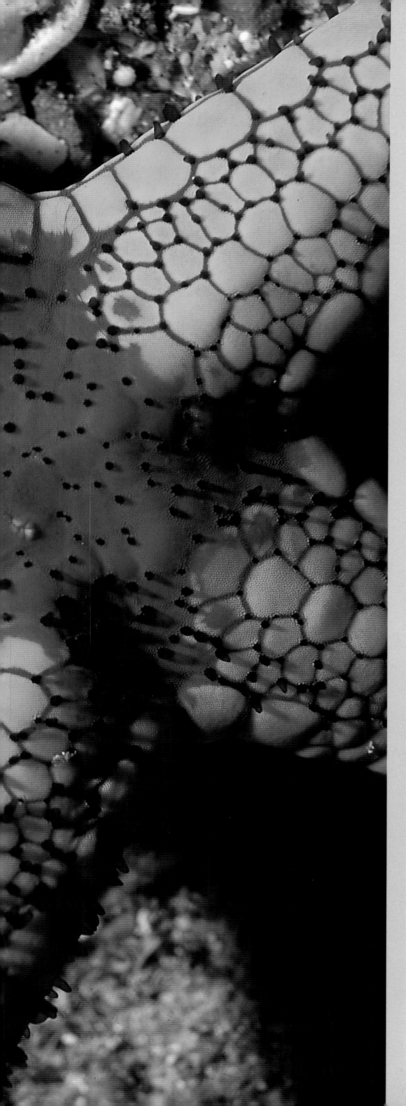

Contents

Breathing
Underwater

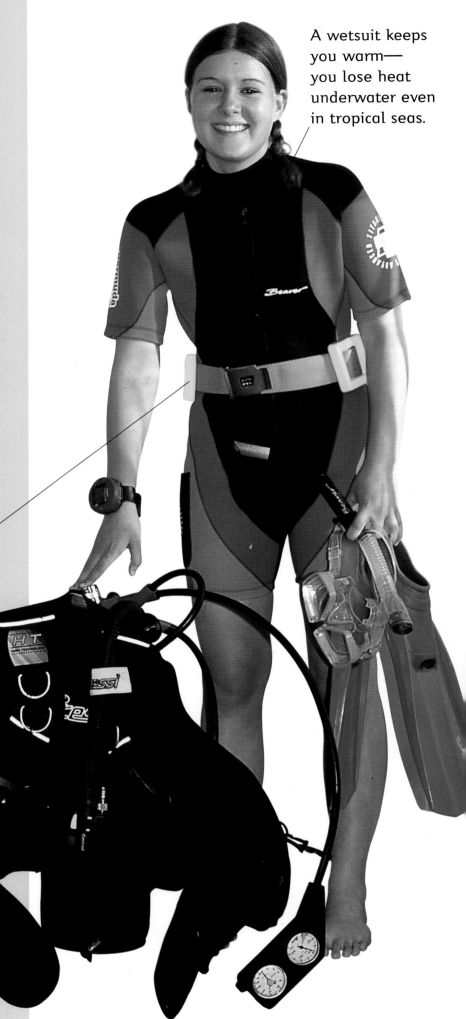

A wetsuit keeps you warm— you lose heat underwater even in tropical seas.

The sea is an important, magical part of the world. It covers nearly three-quarters of the Earth's surface, yet it is largely unknown. A huge variety of life teems in the oceans, from tiny microscopic plants to the largest animal that has ever existed, the blue whale. Different plants and animals live in cold or warm water, and at different depths. Imagine what strange lives they must lead, totally surrounded by water instead of air!

A weight belt has lead weights to counteract the buoyancy of the wetsuit.

We have explored much of the world on land. We have even begun to explore space. But most of us—even if we have traveled across the sea—know very little about what goes on beneath the waves. It is time to explore it properly.

The buoyancy compensator is a jacket that can be inflated and deflated to adjust your buoyancy in water.

Going underwater is a great adventure, but there is one major problem. We cannot breathe there. Sea creatures are able to absorb vital oxygen from the water, through their gills or other parts of their body surface, but we must take an air supply with us. Diving can be dangerous without the right preparation. Before our journey under the sea, we need to be fit, good swimmers, and to have had diving lessons and plenty of practice.

A snorkel is a simple breathing tube.

A mask should fit your face without leaking.

The regulator or demand valve adjusts the air pressure and has a mouthpiece for breathing through.

The air cylinder is filled with air compressed to high pressure.

The buoyancy compensator allows you to control how buoyant you are in the water.

We have to learn to use breathing equipment: snorkel and scuba. A snorkel is a simple tube. You can breathe through it when you are at the surface, without having to lift your head out of the water. There is much more to learn about scuba equipment. The most important parts are the air cylinder, carrying air at high pressure, and the regulator that adjusts the air to breathing pressure. It takes training to use this safely underwater.

Depth and time can be measured by a computer, or by a depth gauge and a waterproof watch.

Snorkeling and scuba diving each have their own advantages and disadvantages. With snorkeling there is no bulky, heavy equipment, but with scuba gear we can stay below for much longer. We are about to enter an alien environment. We will be spending hours face to face with fishes in their own world. Swimming about with them, we may even begin to feel like fishes ourselves!

Fins make swimming easier.

Map of the *Journey*

The best place for a journey under the sea is in safe, calm, clean, warm waters that are teeming with life. There are so many ideal places in the tropics, it is hard to choose just one, but we have heard that Indonesia's wonderful sea life will amaze us. This is where we have decided to make our journey.

Our expedition starts with a long flight, a change of planes, then another flight. Every hour takes us closer to the tropical islands of Indonesia. At last we arrive. As we step out, the bright sunshine dazzles us and a blast of hot, moist air hits us. Better not to rush. Take it slowly, everything is exhausting at first. The airport is noisy and bustling with local people and tourists, and it is a big relief to climb into the back of a waiting jeep and speed away through the countryside. We will soon be at the coast. Under the sea lie some of the world's finest coral reefs. This is where our real adventure begins.

Pygmy seahorse reef

Sea anemone city

Muck dive

Bay

Shallow coral garden

Jett

Dive center

Manta rays

Small island

Turtle nesting beach

Surrounding reef

Tiny island

Steep reef wall

Night dive site

Coral reefs

Sea-grass bed

N
W E
S

Arriving
at the Coast

The road winds past villages and farms. Finally it peters out into a narrow winding track that leads to a small seaside village in a quiet bay. The jeep swings round the last bend above the bay and suddenly, in a gap between the trees, we catch our first glimpse of the sea! It looks so inviting, a calm expanse of deep turquoise. What secrets lie waiting to be discovered here?

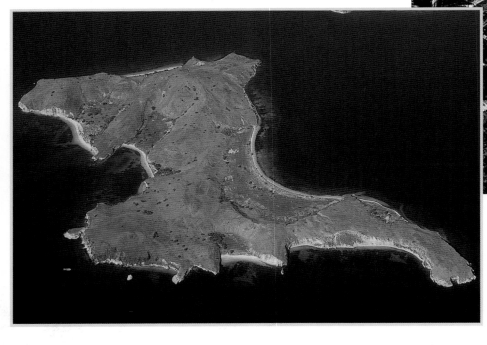

◄ The plane flies over island after island as it nears its destination.

Climbing out of the jeep, we take in the sights, sounds, and smells. As we walk around, we notice how important the sea is to the people living here. Small fishing boats are lined up at the water's edge ready for the night's fishing expedition. Makeshift stalls at a fish market display last night's catch. There are many different kinds of fish, but none of them looks like anything we have seen at our local fish shop.

Village children are jumping into the sea off a jetty, laughing and splashing each other. That looks like fun, but there's no time now—our first job is to find a dive center with a good guide. People we speak to point out one at the far end of the sandy beach. The sun is beating down, but a fringe of coconut palms gives welcome shade. It's only a short walk to reach it.

◀ Down in the bay, the dive center is our base for exploring under the sea.

Several wooden huts built on short stilts are clustered in between the palms. The biggest building is the dive center itself. Smaller huts are for sleeping in. This looks an ideal base for our diving adventure. A boatload of divers is just returning to the shore. They jump out onto the beach, chatting excitedly about the dive they have just been on. With them is their dive guide, Dedi. We go and meet him.

Dedi listens to our plans, and agrees to take us diving. First we must show him our diving qualifications. Then he says the two of us can join the small group that is going out in the boat tomorrow. We can't wait to get in the water, so he suggests that we go for a snorkel around the jetty this afternoon.

▼ The dive boat, like local fishing boats, has an outrigger on each side to keep it stable.

9

Into the
Water

Snorkeling is a great way to explore shallow water. We can look down into the water while breathing through the tube, or take a breath, duck down and do short dives. Dedi sends his young helper to guide us. He will point out creatures that live around the jetty, and he warns us not to touch any of them. Some may be venomous, but they won't harm us if we're just looking.

Standing on the sandy beach, at the water's edge beside the jetty, we put on mask and snorkel then wade into the sea, put on our fins, and start swimming. We are under the water at last! Beneath the jetty it is gloomy, but nearer the edges shafts of light filter through, and outside the sun sparkles through the shallow water onto a stretch of sand. Looking down, we see dozens of fish swimming around. They seem larger and closer than they really are.

◄ The shortfin lionfish is extraordinary but venomous—so don't touch!

◀ Striped catfish swim away faster than a lionfish, but they are venomous too.

As we dive toward the fish they dart away, startled by our sudden approach. They have streamlined bodies and fins. Not all animals swim like this, and many rest or move around on the sea bed. Each time we duck underwater something new catches our attention. If only we could stay down longer. Just as we're getting close enough for a good look, we have to surface to take a breath. We'd never have guessed at all the life down here! Even the jetty's supporting posts are covered with tangled sponges and corals. These make good perches for other creatures, too. Dedi's helper points out an astonishing-looking lionfish, and a frogfish too.

How quickly the afternoon has gone! It's time to call it a day. Back on shore we head for our hut, and after supper we soon fall asleep, our minds whirling with jumbled watery pictures from the underwater world.

▲ Looking back up at the surface, it seems like a barrier between two worlds.

▶ This frogfish has found an ideal perch, on a sponge-encrusted jetty post.

A Meadow
under the Sea

Next morning, we help Dedi to load snorkeling and diving gear onto the boat and head a few miles up the coast to a shallow sea-grass bed. This is home to an amazing array of fish and other animals. Some live here all their lives, others just while they are young, until they are big enough to venture out onto the open reef.

◀ The blue sea star feeds using the mouth in the middle of its underside.

Dedi jumps into the water, and we follow him to what looks like an underwater meadow. It is! Sea grasses are true grasses like those on your lawn, except that they grow in shallow sunlit waters. The grass ripples gently in the slight current.

Immediately in view is a shoal of small silvery fish swimming above the sea grass, but the blades of grass provide cover and food for many other creatures. We dive down to see them more clearly. Some, on bare patches of sand and rubble, are easier to spot.

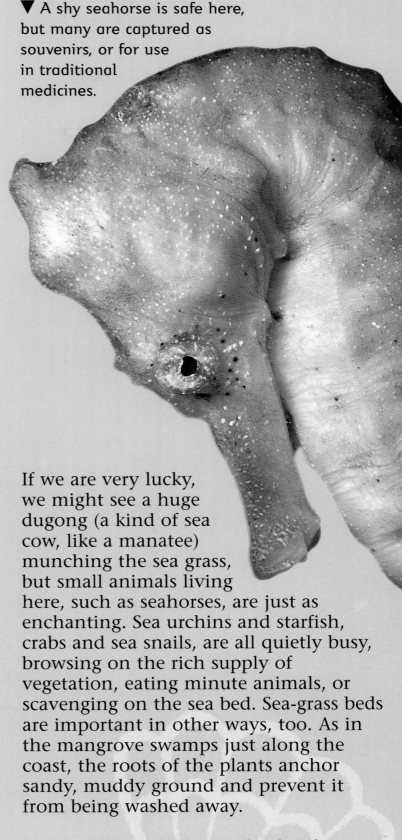

▼ A shy seahorse is safe here, but many are captured as souvenirs, or for use in traditional medicines.

◀ Sea grass is a haven for small fish, young and old.

▲ This dazzling sea urchin is out in the open, but needle-like spines protect it.

If we are very lucky, we might see a huge dugong (a kind of sea cow, like a manatee) munching the sea grass, but small animals living here, such as seahorses, are just as enchanting. Sea urchins and starfish, crabs and sea snails, are all quietly busy, browsing on the rich supply of vegetation, eating minute animals, or scavenging on the sea bed. Sea-grass beds are important in other ways, too. As in the mangrove swamps just along the coast, the roots of the plants anchor sandy, muddy ground and prevent it from being washed away.

We could stay all day in this lovely, tranquil place, but it is time to swim back to the boat for the next step of the journey.

A Shallow Coral Garden

After lunch on board, the boat starts up and we head out to sea. Ten minutes later, the engine cuts and Dedi secures the line to a buoy. He gives us a dive-briefing, telling us about the site—a coral reef—and some of the things we'll see. We look over the side. The water is so clear that we can easily see the bottom, about six yards below.

This time we are going to scuba dive, wearing an air cylinder. The equipment feels heavy and uncomfortable as we sit on the side of the boat waiting for the signal to roll into the water, but when we're under it seems weightless. What a relief!

The shallow reef stretches before us like a gently sloping underwater rock garden, except that the rocks are living coral. Large corals are everywhere, some solid and lumpy, others bushy and branching, or flat like a table. Rays of light play on them as we follow Dedi, swimming just above the reef. Mind the fins! A careless kick could damage corals. Divers are not allowed to touch coral—or even to wear gloves.

▶ Not flowers but animals: each is a coral polyp with a limestone skeleton.

▲ This soft coral has tiny pale limestone ribs all over its branches, instead of a skeleton inside.

Coral reefs form only in warm, sunlit seas. They are the build-up of the limestone skeletons of many small individual creatures, called polyps. Over thousands of years, tiny "bricks" pile up, making huge structures. The resulting reefs are brilliant, underwater "gardens" that are home to thousands of different animals and plants.

Corals may look like plants, but actually they are animals. Within their bodies are microscopic single-celled plants, which help corals to produce enough limestone to make a reef.

We seem to see corals of every shape and color imaginable. Stony corals (the reef builders) are hard but brittle. Others, that do not build reefs, are soft, leathery, or have skeletons of horn.

▲ It's a riot of life and color down here. The reef is a breathtaking sight.

Life on the Reef

▲ Eating plankton from the water fattens these small fish— for a bigger one's dinner.

Everywhere, tiny fish are swarming around the corals, darting for cover in between the branches when a larger fish, or a diver, comes too close. Other fish swim away before we can get a good look at them. Now we remember Dedi's advice in the dive-briefing: swim slowly and avoid making a sudden move, then the fish will not be so nervous. It works!

A beautiful fish is hovering alongside a clump of coral and we hover in front of it, admiring its bright colors. Those spots look as if they've been painted on! Now Dedi catches sight of something moving nearby. He swims slowly toward it.

A fantastic long creature is gaping out of a hole in the reef. A blue snake? No, a moray eel. It looks as if it's going to bite, but this fish is only gulping in water, to get oxygen from it.

There is so much to see here! Fish and other creatures of every shape, color, and size thrive in these shallow waters, where there is warmth, light, and plenty of food. The coral reef is an ecosystem—a community of animals and plants whose lives are linked together. They depend on each other, and on the place where they live, for all their needs.

There are lots of good sheltering places among the corals, and demand for them is high. Out in the open, life is dangerous. The sea is a hunting ground, and size is important in the game of eat or be eaten. How large you are often determines what you can eat, and what can eat you! But not always. Some large fish feed on tiny plankton floating in the water, and parrotfish, even yard-long ones, graze on minute seaweeds.

We glide from one patch of corals to the next, stopping to peer closely at them so we don't miss anything. In a single, heart-stopping moment we witness the death of a small fish, snapped up by a sturdier one. Feeding is going on all around us, but it's mostly unnoticed. Now we are coming to a bend in the reef. There is just time to find out what lies behind it.

► The leafy nose moray eel senses prey approaching. Those nostrils pick up vibrations in the water.

◄ With eyes on stalks keeping a lookout, the hermit crab puts its pincers out to scavenge for titbits.

Survival
on the Reef

The reef curves round, bringing into view a shoal of fish, out from the shelter of corals. As we pass they stream off, but they don't go far, and soon regroup in their favorite patch. It's like watching a ballet! These fish swim as one, all facing the same way, and keeping exactly the same distance apart.

The shoal could almost be a single fish. A prowling predator thinks that too and moves on by, unable to pick out just one.

It seems so peaceful here, yet danger waits at every turn for unwary creatures. Keeping out of harm's way seems sensible. But there is more room in the open, as well as some of the best opportunities for feeding. So, how can animals live out and about and stay safe?

◄ The tentacles (or gills) of this tube worm have earned it the name "Christmas tree worm."

▲ Once danger has passed, the porcupinefish deflates with a sigh of relief, and its spines lie flat.

Sea creatures have solved that dilemma in more ingenious ways than anyone could imagine. An alarmed porcupinefish swallows water and blows itself up like a spiky soccerball. Not a good meal!

Heavy shells protect clams, but they need to open to feed and breathe. Tubes encase some worms, except for their feathery tentacles. Both clam and worm sense our approach and take immediate action. The clam's shell swings shut, the worm pulls its tentacles back into the tube, and this worm even closes its tube with a spiked trapdoor! Other animals sting. Dedi warns us not to touch anything.

Time has flown. Have we really been underwater for a whole hour? That stretch of reef ahead will have to wait until tomorrow.

▲ Twenty pairs of eyes, but one shoal. These small emperors stick close together for safety.

◄ The shell of a giant clam gapes open, revealing the soft folds of flesh of the living animal.

A World of Color

We wake early, eager to get going again. This time, the boat takes us further along the reef. We drop into the water and descend to the shallow sea bed. Dedi stops to inspect a patch of coral rubble. There! He has found one right away. And another. Little splashes of color stand out here and there. Can these be sea slugs? They are so bright and beautiful!

This is a good place to look for colorful sea creatures. But why are they so brightly colored? It can help animals of the same species to recognize each other, but what if they are seen by predators? Startling colors and patterns can also help animals to defend themselves. A spot that looks like an eye confuses an enemy; other markings warn attackers to back off. Bold colors often spell danger, like the black-and-yellow stripes of a wasp. It's just the same in the undersea world.

▲ The strong colors of the sea slugs are startlingly beautiful.

► Don't mess with me! That's what this spectacular lionfish display means.

▲ This sea slug's black-and-yellow markings warn of the toxic chemicals in its skin.

▶ Sticky tentacles of the flame file shell can break off if touched, and the mollusk swims safely away.

Hundreds of different kinds of sea slugs live in these seas, each with its own pattern, like an assortment of brightly wrapped candies. Don't try to eat one! Many sea slugs are poisonous. A fish that tastes unpleasant chemicals on the slug's skin soon learns to leave it, and anything that looks like it, alone. Most small mollusks, other than slugs, have shells, a single one for snails and a hinged pair of shell-halves for clams and their relatives.

◀ The exposed plume of gills gives sea slugs their other name— nudibranch—which means "naked gill."

We've searched this patch thoroughly. Time to move on, there's more to see yet. Look! Just ahead, by that coral, a spectacular lionfish is spreading its patterned fins, like a fan. This is a warning flag, telling all comers to keep their distance. The long spines will inject poison if they pierce skin.

Octopus
and Cuttlefish

A small octopus slinks along the sand, looking for a place to settle in for a while. It finds a couple of empty sea shells. Those will do! Octopuses like to hide in holes for most of the day, saving their energy for hunting crabs and small fish at night, but you can sometimes see them on the move from one retreat to the next.

A head pops up from a burrow—another octopus. It looks around, the coast is clear and the animal climbs out, its eight arms flowing onto the sea bed. Octopuses have soft, flexible bodies and can squeeze in and out of incredibly tight places. They are ingenious, too; octopuses in captivity have even learned to unscrew lids to get at food.

▲ Are these shells big enough? The octopus will have to pull them closer if it wants to escape notice.

Dedi leads us up the reef to a spot where he saw a pair of cuttlefish the other day. Sure enough, they are still there, getting ready to mate. As we swim near they react warily, and one of them raises two arms in front, like horns. Now the cuttlefish are flashing waves of color over their bodies. Amazing!

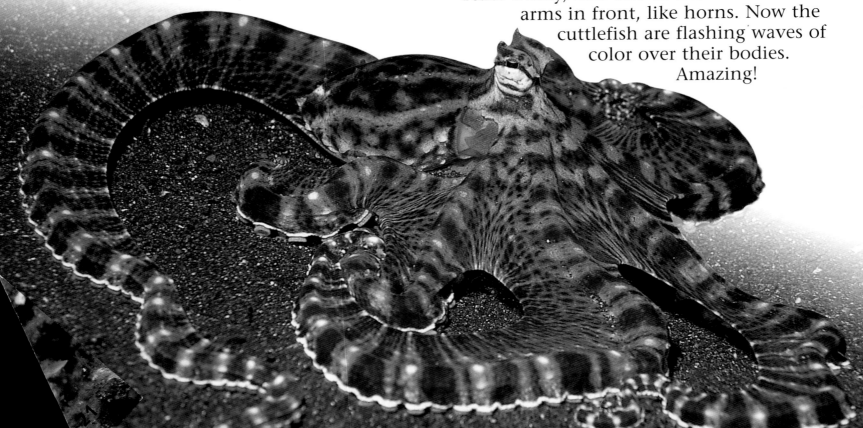

▲ The flamboyant cuttlefish is so colorful it could almost be a large sea slug.

Cuttlefish (and octopuses and squids) have pigment cells all over their skin, as dots of different colors. These dots can swell or shrink so rapidly that it looks like a pulse of color. That's not all. Cuttlefish can make their skin go spiky or smooth, and strike poses with their arms. Put all these tricks together and you have a fantastic show. It's more than a show—the animals are sending out signals. Scientists have managed to interpret some of their language and it is surprisingly complex. The message from our cuttlefish seems clear though: "go away!"

If that's not enough, any of these animals can do a disappearing act by sending out a smokescreen of ink and making a jet-propelled escape. A mimic octopus makes its escape in another way. It can make itself look like a whole range of inedible creatures. It's hard to believe that such lively, intelligent animals are related to slugs and snails.

◄ Cuttlefish, octopuses, and squids are thought to be the brainiest of all invertebrate animals.

◄ Disturb this mimic octopus and it might pretend to be a sea snake, stingray, lionfish, or flounder.

Cunning
Camouflage

A coral reef is full of surprises. Brightly colored creatures are easy to spot, but Dedi's sharp eyes pick out others that are not so obvious. He points at something, a small rock? No, look again, it's a scorpionfish lying still on the sea bed. Its lumpy shape and knobbly, speckled skin fooled us into thinking it was just coral rubble!

What's Dedi pointing at? A lump of sponge? No, it's a frogfish. It lures its prey by waving a "fishing rod," a spine with a fleshy tassel at the tip. As we turn to go, a decorator crab sidles by, with a roof garden on its back. It has tufts of weed and blobs of sponge stuck all over it. Some animals really do wear their camouflage!

▲ Looking like a bad-tasting sponge is a good idea for a frogfish that wants to be left alone.

▶ Frills and flaps of skin are part of the scorpionfish's disguise.

▲ Is my camouflage working? The best bet for a hungry scorpionfish is to keep as still as a rock.

Slow-moving animals cannot easily escape when a predator moves in for the kill, so one of their best defenses is to avoid being seen. Their camouflage makes them blend into the scenery. Attackers can use camouflage too. A scorpionfish saves energy while waiting and watching for the next meal to swim by. Time it right, take a big gulp, and snap up a small creature that will never know what hit it.

◀ Peeping out from beneath an eyelid like a tasseled curtain, a crocodilefish secretly watches its neighbors.

Anemonefish are also called clownfish, and looking at their large downturned mouths, poster-paint colors, and "playful" antics it is easy to see why. With a flurry of fins they disappear under the tentacles, only to pop out unexpectedly in a different spot. Another waggle and they are gone again. They are so amusing, but hide-and-seek is a game of life and death if a predator is watching them. Anemones' tentacles make a good hiding place. Their sting keeps predators away, but anemonefish are not stung. They are covered in protective slime.

◄ Brush against this anemone, and you risk a sting from the tentacles *and* a nip from the bold little fish.

▼ A few spots of color make the glass-like body of this anemone shrimp just visible.

Living Together

Dedi leads the way through an underwater city of sea anemones. Huge anemones among the corals are plump and velvety, like cushions crowned with tentacles. Smaller ones crop up in the sand, like flowers in a desert. Best of all, bold-colored fish dart in and out of their tentacles.

▲ This porcelain crab plays it safe, ready to take cover between folds of the anemone's flesh.

A pair of small claws waves out from the tentacles. A couple of tiny porcelain crabs have made their home here, too. As we watch, we notice some shrimps dancing on the tentacles. We nearly missed them, they are so tiny and transparent. Living together suits many creatures, and makes for some unlikely partners. Shrimps live with all sorts of animals: anemones and corals, sea urchins and starfish are just some of them. They even share a burrow with gobies.

A fish gapes wide while a shrimp scampers around its mouth. This shrimp is a cleaner, which nibbles dead skin and parasites off fish to keep them healthy. Dedi removes his demand valve and poses like the fish. A shrimp leaps onto his lips to clean his teeth! Shrimps are not the only cleaners here. Nearby a small fish, a wrasse, is cleaning a larger one.

▶ A redmouth grouper gets cleaned, and leaves its cleaner shrimp unharmed.

Hidden
Creatures

If you swim over a coral reef just taking in the beautiful scenery, you will miss an incredible number of tiny animals of all shapes and colors. Dedi says we must move much more slowly to see them. We must practice good buoyancy control, so we can swim up very close to the corals and hold our position without knocking into them.

▶ It's hard to tell where coral ends and crab begins on this soft coral.

Inspecting everything closely brings such rewards! Tiny creatures hide in the most unexpected places. We peer at a sea cucumber. It moves sluggishly over the sea bed, looking more like a giant caterpillar than a starfish, its true relative. Scuttling over its plump body are a few minute crabs and shrimps that live with it.

Another relative of starfish, a feather star, has other kinds of shrimps concealed in its feather-like arms. They are so well hidden even Dedi has to search hard for them.

▶ A soft coral might be hiding dozens of tiny crabs—you'd never know from this distance.

28

▲ This shrimp has its
ideal home, the wiry
stem of a black coral.

All over the reef there are special
partnerships between creatures. Corals
and other big partners provide a home
and protection for their little partners.
Not content with that, little partners
scavenge scraps of food off them, and
sometimes nibble them. Some may
give nothing in return. Others may
help their big partner by eating its
parasites. Small occupants
often look as if they are bits
of their partners. The spines
and color of a soft coral
crab disguise it perfectly
on a branch of soft coral.

We've been diving over
an hour, but we've only
covered a short distance.
You don't need to travel
far when exploring these
miniature worlds.

◄ An emperor shrimp rides
in comfort on the skin of its
partner, a sea cucumber.

29

In Search of the
Seahorse

Even though Dedi dives on these reefs every day, he still finds new things. He has recently discovered a spot where some rare creatures live, and today he is taking us there. He leads the way slowly down a sloping reef, deeper than we've been before.

▶ Knobs on the pygmy seahorse look just like the polyps on a sea fan's branches.

▼ A feather star perches in the open, its arms straining tiny morsels from the water currents.

The light is a little dimmer here, but our eyes soon adjust. Large sea fans stand out from the sea bed. Their lacy network of fine branches strains tiny particles of food from the water currents. Dedi shines his flashlight on them, and suddenly their bright colors glow before us. We can only stay at this depth for a few minutes more without risking decompression sickness. But Dedi is beckoning us over. He points at something, but we can't see what.

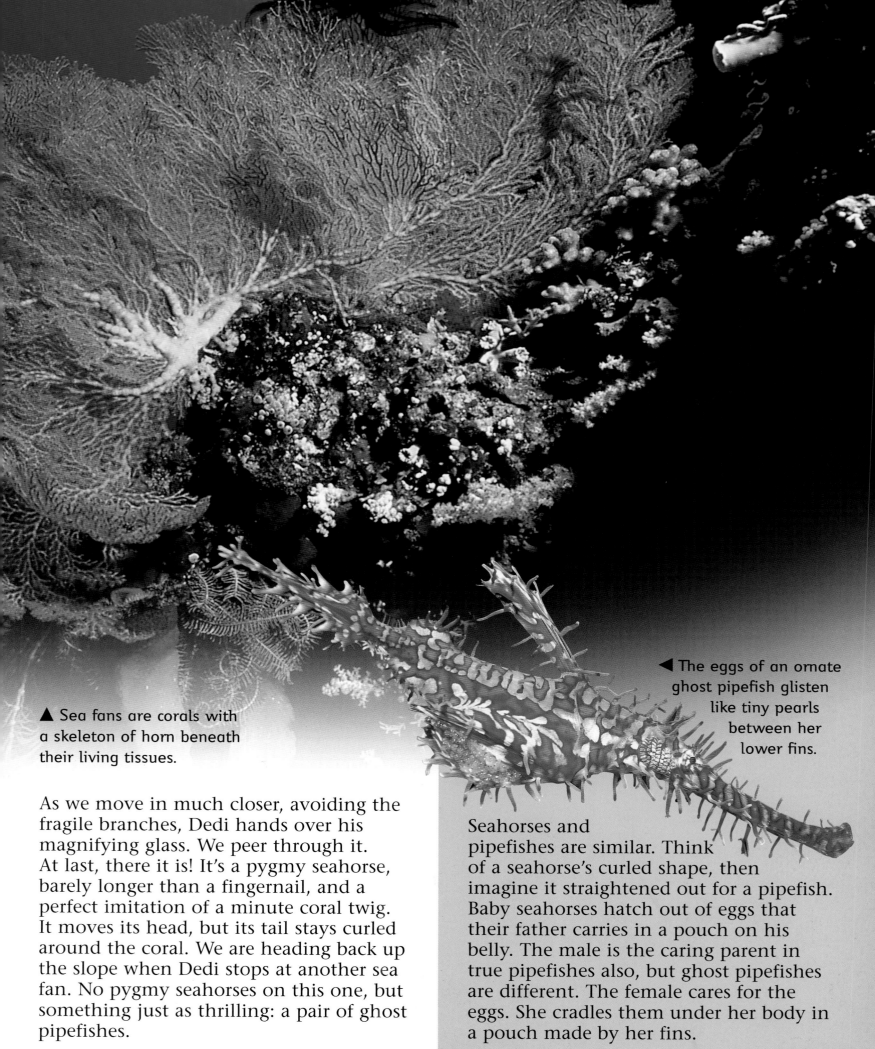

▲ Sea fans are corals with a skeleton of horn beneath their living tissues.

◀ The eggs of an ornate ghost pipefish glisten like tiny pearls between her lower fins.

As we move in much closer, avoiding the fragile branches, Dedi hands over his magnifying glass. We peer through it. At last, there it is! It's a pygmy seahorse, barely longer than a fingernail, and a perfect imitation of a minute coral twig. It moves its head, but its tail stays curled around the coral. We are heading back up the slope when Dedi stops at another sea fan. No pygmy seahorses on this one, but something just as thrilling: a pair of ghost pipefishes.

Seahorses and pipefishes are similar. Think of a seahorse's curled shape, then imagine it straightened out for a pipefish. Baby seahorses hatch out of eggs that their father carries in a pouch on his belly. The male is the caring parent in true pipefishes also, but ghost pipefishes are different. The female cares for the eggs. She cradles them under her body in a pouch made by her fins.

A Night
Dive

After a busy day on the reef, we're going back for a night dive! We're excited, but also a little apprehensive about diving in the dark. So we're glad when Dedi says that we will start at dusk. We're going to see a spectacular event that only happens then: mandarinfish mating. With fresh batteries in our flashlights, we're ready to go.

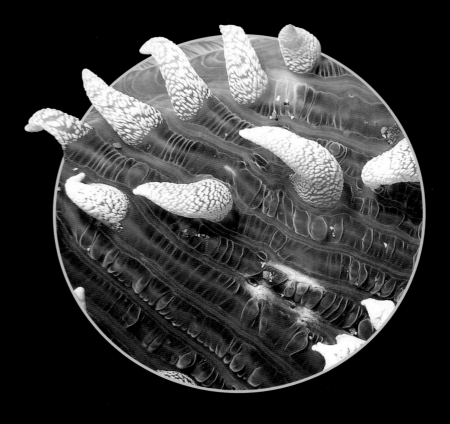

▲ A stony coral extends its tentacles for feeding at night.

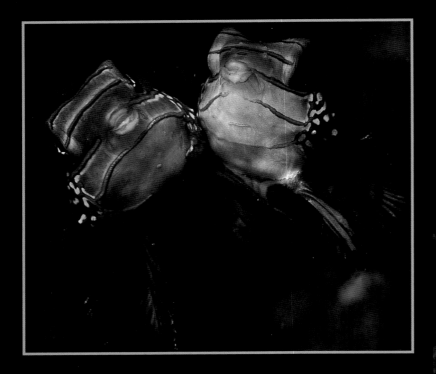

◀ Dancing cheek to cheek: a pair of mandarinfish get ready to mate.

The sinking Sun still spreads plenty of light above water, but below the surface it is already getting gloomy. By the time we are stationed on the sand around a patch of coral, we need our flashlights on. As their beams play on the corals an amazing thing happens. A small brightly colored fish wriggles out and almost bumps into another one. Mandarinfish have started their courtship.

The fish move side by side, pressing close. They beat their fins and rise up slowly together in the water. Their courtship dance is entrancing—but suddenly the spell breaks. The fish split and dive separately back into the corals. They have mated. Again and again, pairs rise up. The action builds up, then dies down. The session is over for this evening.

Our night dive is only just beginning. As we swim over the reef we are surrounded by blackness, apart from the pools of light thrown by our flashlights. Shadowy outlines of coral boulders loom up, and brilliant patches of color appear with startling suddenness. That dark shape beneath an overhang turns out to be a crimson fish.

▲ Even though helmet gurnards are encased in box-like armor, they can be wary, but at night they are very approachable.

Other sea animals are out and about now, searching for food. Crabs and lobsters crawl out of their daytime hiding places. Shrimps with eyes that gleam like beads skip about in rock crevices. Nocturnal fish are hunting, while day-active fish have found sleeping places in corals or the sand.

A bright light flashing on the mooring line guides us back to the boat. Motoring to shore, we watch the inky water ripple past. Small flashes of light sparkle at the surface. Dedi explains that tiny plankton are producing this glowing night light, called bioluminescence. They rise up from deeper water in the dark. At last, the boat pulls in to the jetty and we stumble ashore, tired but exhilarated. We will sleep well tonight!

◀ A wood louse crossed with a mechanical digger? No, it's a slipper lobster with a pair of shovel-like plates in front.

33

A Muck
Dive

The following morning we suit up, ready to go diving for the last time from this island. Dedi promises something really unusual. Heading down, the sea bed looks hazy and the bottom seems dull and featureless—just mud, gravel, and black sand. Our first impression is disappointment after all our beautiful coral reef dives. Has Dedi made a mistake?

▶ A snake eel burrows into the sand with its tough, pointed tail tip.

▲ Flatfish have both eyes on the same side of their head, the left side for this one—a left-eyed flounder.

But already he has found something and he waves us over. A spiny devilfish! This extraordinary creature is crawling across the sand on "fingertips" (actually parts of its fins). Watch out, there's another one. We almost knelt on its venomous spines! The animals here are stranger than anything we have ever seen. Some are so well hidden by skin growths looking like a covering of moss, that we would never spot them without Dedi. Here and there, heads of small creatures pop out of the sand. They duck back in if we get too close.

A large stingray flaps its body in the silt, sending up a cloud. When the water clears the ray has gone. Not quite! Its eyes are sticking out of the silt, watching us. We dare not spend too long looking at any one thing, for fear of missing the next. We won't forget this dive—no doubt! Back on shore, we are bound for other islands and new places to dive. A tiny cabin will be our home for several nights, or maybe a mattress on deck, swaying under the stars.

► Not much of a swimmer, the spiny devilfish prefers to scuttle along the sea bed on its fins.

Deeper
Water

As we stand on deck, looking back to shore, our island gets smaller and smaller, until we cannot make it out anymore and all around us is open sea. But now, ahead, a speck appears on the horizon. As it grows larger, we see a cluster of trees above a white strip of beach. Dedi calls us to get ready—this tiny island is the perfect place to stop for a dive.

▼ We descend the reef wall encrusted with colorful animals.

Underwater, a short swim takes us across a shallow reef. All seems familiar. But what's this? A cliff edge? We are at a "drop-off," the top of a steep wall. We swim out a little way, look down—and catch our breath. Will we fall? Fish are swimming so far beneath us, way down in the ever-deeper blue. Our eyes follow them down, but the water holds us up. It is an amazing feeling, there's no need to be scared.

Just off the wall, shoaling fish are lining up in the current. These are active hunters that patrol the drop-off, and they can swim fast. Their shape tells us that. Their streamlined bodies are propelled by powerful forked tails.

As we swim slowly down the wall, we do start to sink, and need to press the direct-feed button that puts air in our buoyancy compensator, just enough to keep us from either sinking or rising.

◄ Golden sergeants are often seen alongside outer reef walls.

Deeper down, the light gradually becomes dimmer and everything appears more blue. Water absorbs light, taking out the red end of the spectrum first, but shining a light on things brings back their color. Dedi's flashlight shows up surprising colors on the reef wall, yellow and red patches of sponges and sea squirts.

Dedi is monitoring the dive time carefully. Stay too long at depth and there is a risk of decompression sickness. He raises his thumb, the signal to ascend. We swim slowly upward, to continue the dive at a shallower level.

▲ These shoaling jacks are hunters, built to chase and catch other fish in the open sea.

▶ Sea squirts live attached to the reef, drawing water in through one hole and letting it flow out the other.

A Passing Shadow

A slight current carries us drifting along the wall. It feels as if we are flying. Suddenly Dedi wheels round and points at a shadow passing nearby. It is the dark torpedo-like shape of a shark. Thankfully it has no interest in us, and cruises by—what a thrilling moment!

▲ The largest shark is the whale shark, a gentle giant that strains small fish out of the water.

As the shark speeds away, we gaze after it, admiring its power and grace. Sharks are built to swim fast. They are streamlined and have strong forked tails, like the shoaling fishes we have just passed. In other ways they are different. Sharks' skeletons are made of a gristle called cartilage, not of bone. Cartilage is lighter and more elastic than bone, and makes swimming in the open ocean easier. Other fish have swim bladders, built-in floats filled with gas. Instead, many sharks have large oily livers that help their buoyancy.

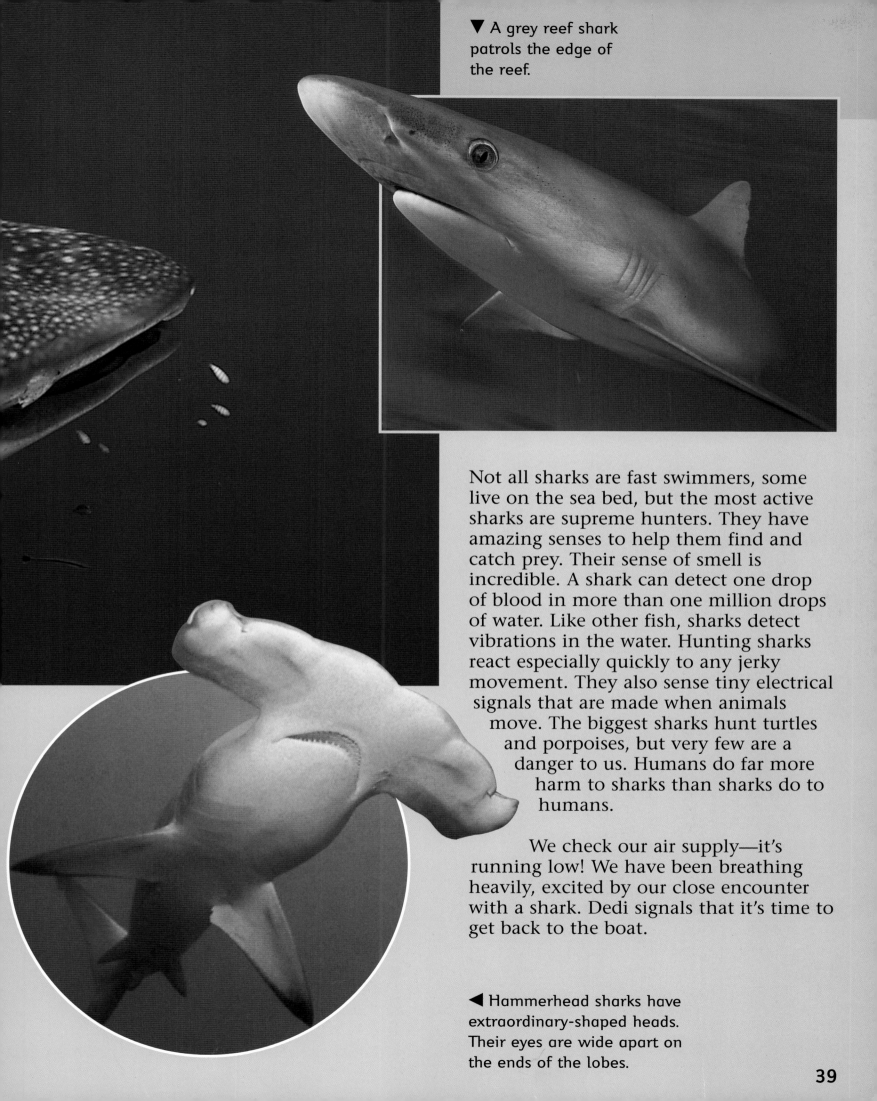

▼ A grey reef shark patrols the edge of the reef.

Not all sharks are fast swimmers, some live on the sea bed, but the most active sharks are supreme hunters. They have amazing senses to help them find and catch prey. Their sense of smell is incredible. A shark can detect one drop of blood in more than one million drops of water. Like other fish, sharks detect vibrations in the water. Hunting sharks react especially quickly to any jerky movement. They also sense tiny electrical signals that are made when animals move. The biggest sharks hunt turtles and porpoises, but very few are a danger to us. Humans do far more harm to sharks than sharks do to humans.

We check our air supply—it's running low! We have been breathing heavily, excited by our close encounter with a shark. Dedi signals that it's time to get back to the boat.

◀ Hammerhead sharks have extraordinary-shaped heads. Their eyes are wide apart on the ends of the lobes.

Manta Rays

The tiny island is out of sight, far behind us, as our boat nears the island we have been heading for. It is a special place where manta rays can be seen. They live mostly in the open sea, but sometimes visit coral reefs. They come to this island to feed and to breed. Will they be here today?

Just as the engine cuts out, one of the crew gives a shout. We rush across the deck to look out the other side. A dark diamond shape ripples the surface before diving out of sight. Our first manta! We race each other to suit up and jump in. The shallow reef around this island has a sandy channel. We swim a little way along it until Dedi signals us to stop. We drop gently onto the sand and wait. "Don't move," Dedi had said, "and they will come to you." We strain our eyes trying to catch a distant glimpse of a manta under water. Suddenly the first one appears, followed by several more, gliding straight toward us. The huge rays swoop above us: nine, no, ten of them.

► A big manta ray may be more than 6 yards wide and weigh more than 2,200 pounds.

For 20 minutes the mantas circle the area. They seem to fly through the water with slow, graceful flaps of their immense outstretched fins—just like wings. These rays are a good 3 yards across, and they can be larger still. Seen from above, they are dark steel-grey. As they glide slowly overhead they show a vast expanse of white belly.

► Being dark on top and pale underneath makes an animal less visible in the open sea.

We have never seen anything like these fantastic rays. They have a strange pair of lobes sticking out in front. After the dive Dedi tells us about them. Unlike most rays, mantas feed on plankton, which they catch near the surface. As the rays cruise along, their lobes guide the food toward their open mouths.

Stepping ashore, we look back for a last sight of a manta's fins breaking the surface of the water.

▶ Down on the sand you can see other kinds of rays, like this bluespotted ribbontail ray.

Reptiles
of the Sea

After lunch we explore the strip of beach surrounding the densely forested island. Dedi stops at a set of tracks crossing the firm sand. Turtles! They come ashore at night to lay eggs, but now is a good time to look for them in the sea. We hurry to get our diving gear on.

Ten minutes into the dive, a turtle swims out from the reef top. It is heading this way fast, propelled by large front flippers, rowing like oars.

▼ Green turtles are mainly vegetarian, eating seaweeds and sea grasses.

▲ Hawksbill turtles use their beak-like mouths to pry out crabs and scrape sponges and sea squirts off rocks.

The turtle comes very close, before veering off into open water. It's a male: his tail sticks out well behind his shell. Another turtle is swimming toward us, a female, with a short tail. She swims up to the surface, where she stays for a couple of minutes. Turtles cannot breathe underwater and must come up for air. If you are watching from a boat, a floating turtle looks rather like a log. Seen from below, there is no risk of confusion —the turtle's outline is unmistakable. It is incredible to think that turtles much like these have been swimming in the oceans for 90 million years.

▲ Sea turtles are strong swimmers, much more at home in the water than on land.

Turtles spend most of their lives in the sea, but the females lay their eggs on land. Before going to bed, we take a walk along the sand. A low dome shows up ahead. It is a large green turtle, dragging herself slowly up the beach by her flippers. She must weigh well over 200 pounds. What an effort she has on land! This is a difficult and dangerous time for her.

We stand back to watch without disturbing her. She starts to dig a nest with her flippers, throwing sand behind her. Tears run down her face, but she is crying only to get rid of salt from her body. She will lay a hundred or more eggs, each with a round leathery shell, before covering the nest with sand. When the young turtles hatch out, they will race for the sea.

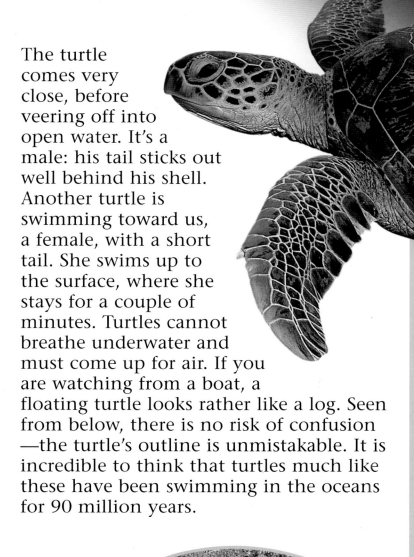

◀ The turtle lays her eggs in the sand and then leaves them to hatch on their own.

Seas in
Danger

Sunshine wakes us early, but the crew is already up and busy preparing our boat to set off. It stops at the far end of the island. We are making one last dive. This reef is as lovely as any we have seen. It is a thicket of perfect corals, not a branch broken, and teeming with fish.

Boom! The shock wave of a distant explosion shatters the peaceful moment. Fishermen are dynamiting the reef to catch fish. As we swim round the point, an unexpected scene awaits us. Smashed coral lies all along the upper slope of the reef.

▲ Life in a small coastal village revolves around the sea. The villagers need international help to protect it for the future.

▼ A coral reef will take many years to recover from damage by a storm or by blast-fishing.

Coral reefs face many dangers. Fragile corals are easily broken by storms and by people. Not all boat crews are as careful as ours to avoid scraping the reef. Modern developments can also cause damage. Pollution and sediment run into the sea when building sites and industries take over coastlines, and when forests are cut down. Global warming threatens corals. It takes only a few degrees' rise in the sea temperature to kill them.

▼ Large fish, like this humphead wrasse, are vulnerable to overfishing.

▲ Some fish collected by aquarists are endangered. These rare banggai cardinalfish could become extinct.

Overfishing is harming life in the oceans. For thousands of years, people living by the sea have fished by simple methods for the food they need. Taking only small numbers of fish leaves others to breed and keep the stocks going. Modern fishing methods often take so many fish that species cannot recover. Our seas need better care.

Swimming back, we take a last look around before surfacing. Up on deck, we rinse the salt out of our equipment. The bow of the boat points toward the distant coast, many hours from sight, where we started our journey under the sea. We wonder if we will ever again see so many beautiful fish and reefs.

Glossary

aquarist Someone who keeps animals or plants alive in tanks of water.

bioluminescence The glowing light made by some living animals and plants.

buoyancy (neutral) A state where you neither float up nor sink.

buoyancy compensator A jacket that can be inflated and deflated to adjust your buoyancy in water.

camouflage A disguise that helps an animal to hide.

cartilage Gristle, a tough but elastic substance.

cleaner (fish or shrimp) A fish or shrimp that eats parasites and dead skin off other fish and cleans up any wounds they have.

conservation Looking after the environment in order to keep the balance of nature.

corals Kinds of sea animals that are similar to sea anemones but often have a hard skeleton.

demand valve (or regulator) The part of a diver's equipment that adjusts the pressure of the air supply for breathing and supplies it through a mouthpiece.

dive center A place that organizes diving excursions.

diversity The range of different kinds of animals and plants there are living in an area.

ecosystem A community of animals and plants, sharing the same environment, whose lives are linked together.

endangered (species) A species threatened with extinction.

environment Natural surroundings.

gill An organ for breathing in water.

global warming An average increase in the Earth's temperature, which in turn causes changes in climate.

graze To feed on plants such as grass or low-growing seaweeds, cropping them down to the ground or sea bed.

invertebrates Animals without a backbone.

mangroves Trees and shrubs growing in muddy swamps on tropical coasts.

mimic An animal or plant that imitates another.

mollusks A group of invertebrate animals including snails, clams, and others that have shells; the group also includes slugs, octopuses, cuttlefish, and squids.

muck dive A dive where the sea bed is muddy and sandy, but often with lots of interesting creatures.

nocturnal Active at night.

parasite A plant or animal that feeds and lives on or in another living creature.

pigment A chemical substance that gives color to an animal or plant.

plankton Animals and plants that drift in water.

polyps (coral) The individual living animals that make up a colony of corals.

predator An animal that hunts and kills other animals for food.

prey An animal that is killed and eaten by another animal.

reef A ridge of rock in the water, in tropical seas often made up of the hard skeletons of corals.

regulator (or demand valve) The part of a diver's equipment that adjusts the pressure of the air supply for breathing and supplies it through a mouthpiece.

reptile Scaly, cold-blooded animal such as a turtle, snake, lizard, or crocodile.

scavenge To feed on refuse scraps of dead animals or plants.

scuba Self-Contained Underwater Breathing Apparatus; equipment that allows divers to breathe underwater.

sea fan A fan-shaped coral with a horny skeleton.

sea grass A kind of grass that grows on the sea bed.

sea slugs Sea-living mollusks without shells.

sea squirts A group of invertebrate animals that live attached to rocks or other objects in the sea, and often look rather like grapes or small vases.

species A particular type of animal or plant, distinct from other kinds.

spectrum The range of colors that light is made up of; the colors of the spectrum can be seen when light passes through a prism.

swim bladder A built-in float, filled with gas, that many fish have.

symbiosis A partnership between different kinds of animals or plants

living together. Such relationships are beneficial to the animals and plants involved.

tentacle A slender, flexible arm-like part that some animals have, often used for feeling.

toxic Poisonous.

tropics The parts of the globe between two imaginary lines, the Tropic of Cancer and the Tropic of Capricorn; the tropics are hot all year round.

venomous Having a poisonous bite or sting.

Index

Acknowledgments

All photographs by Linda Pitkin, except the following: Tobias Bernhard, cover center, p. 39 top right; Javed Jafferji, Oxford Scientific Films, p. 43 bottom left. Artwork on pp. 6–7 by Sarah Young.

Linda Pitkin would like to thank Rose Chorlton for modeling, and Orca Diving Centre, South London, for the use of equipment and facilities, pp. 4–5. She would also like to thank her husband, Brian, for reading and checking the text.

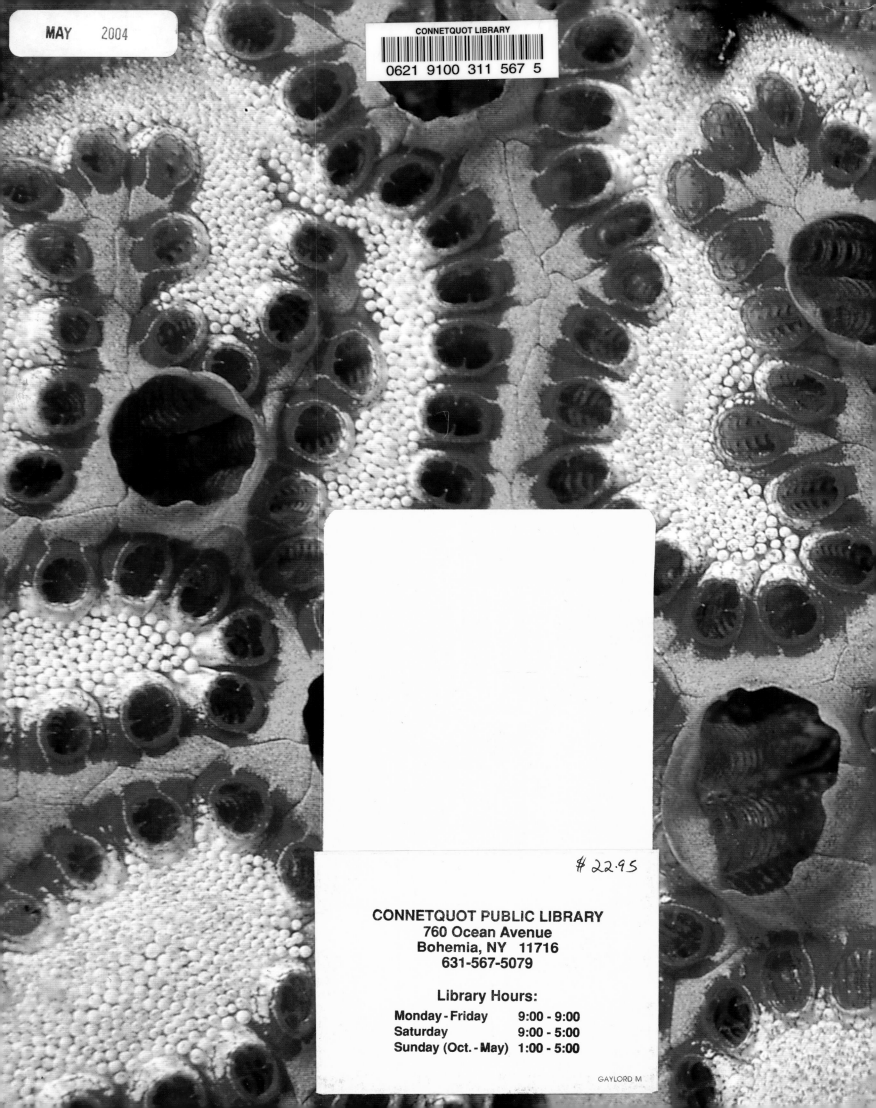